Things Your Dad Always Told You But You Didn't Want To Hear.

by
Carolyn Coats

Thomas Nelson Publishers
Nashville

The easiest way to have your family tree traced is to run for public office.

Nothing good ever happens after midnight.

Cooperation is doing something with a smile that you have to do anyway.

It is unreasonable to expect others to listen to your advice and ignore your example.

When people say
"That's the way the ball
bounces," they're
usually the ones who
dropped it.

One reason for doing the right thing today - is tomorrow.

Some people think the three basic food groups are canned, frozen and take-out.

It is better to teach your children the roots of labor than to hand them the fruits of yours.

If you're not afraid to face the music, you may someday lead the band.

Birds of a feather flock to a newly washed car.

Criticism is the one thing that most of us think is more blessed to give than to receive.

The art of being wise is the art of knowing what to overlook.

Nothing is as hard to do gracefully as getting down off your high horse.

Children have more need of models than of critics.

If you think a woman can't keep a secret, ask one her age.

Every prize

has its price.

Time may be a great healer, but it's a terrible makeup artist.

There is no limit to
what can be accomplished
if we don't mind who
gets the credit.

Robert Woodruff

Before you borrow money from a friend, decide which you need more.

A father is a man who expects his children to be as good as he meant to be.

Mealtime - When teenagers sit down to continue eating.

In life as in golf,
it's the follow through
that makes the
difference.

No farmer ever plowed a field by turning it over in his mind.

It is far better to follow well than to lead poorly.

There comes a time to fish or cut bait.

Things may come
to those who wait,
but only the things
left by those who
hustle. Abraham Lincoln

The best way to keep children home is to make the home atmosphere pleasant and let the air out of their tires.

Don't let the crowd pressure you; Stand for something or you'll fall for anything.

Maturity is the ability to live in peace with that which we cannot change.

It's one thing to lie and another not to talk about your skeletons.

The pessimist sees the difficulty in every opportunity. The optimist sees opportunity in every difficulty.

Common sense is the knack of seeing things as they really are.

The test of our love
for God is the love
we have for one
another.

A diplomat is a person who thinks twice before saying nothing.

Work is the best thing ever invented for killing time.

Anyone can count
the seeds in an apple
but only God can count
the apples in a seed.

We always have time for the things we put first.

Nothing hurts more than having to pay income tax, unless it's not having an income to pay taxes on.

Don't be afraid to trust an unknown future to an all knowing God.

Never do card tricks for the boys you play poker with.

Success is relative.
The more success,
The more relatives.

Every father should remember that one day his children will follow his example instead of his advice.

Watch carefully
those who are good
at what they do.

The more you prepare,
The luckier you get.

You never get a second chance to make a first impression.

Tough times don't last but tough people do.

What you do speaks
so loudly that I can't
hear what you say.

It is not the "IQ" but the "I Will" that is important.

Love doesn't make the world go around but it's what makes the ride worthwhile.

Sometimes you've got to go out on a limb. Isn't that where the fruit is?

Don't depend on a rabbits' foot for luck; remember it didn't work well for the rabbit.

A mistake is only proof that someone was at least trying to accomplish something.

Children are a comfort to us in our old age, and they help us to reach it a lot sooner.

Men of genius are admired;
Men of wealth are envied;
Men of power are feared;
But only men of character
are trusted.

Hard work is the yeast that raises the dough.

People who fly into a rage often make a bad landing.

Leaders are ordinary people with extraordinary determination.

Quitters never win and winners never quit.

The best way to convince fools that they are wrong is to let them have their way.

Repentance is sorrow for the deed, not for being caught.

Opportunity may knock only once but temptation keeps on pounding forever.

Many receive advice,
only the wise profit
from it.

Don't bite the hand that has your allowance in it.

By failing to prepare
You are preparing
to fail.

Benjamin Franklin

Give "Mom" an inch and the whole family goes on a diet.

There would be
fewer divorces if
we tried as hard to
keep our mates as
we did to get them.

If fifty million people say or do a foolish thing, it is still a foolish thing.

No one has a good enough memory to be a successful liar.

Don't ever slam a door you might want to go back in.

Whatever you do in life, never do anything to embarrass the family name.

No man can think clearly when his fists are clenched.

We are only young once, but we can be immature indefinitely.

A good test of peoples character is their behavior when they are wrong.

The grass may be greener on the other side, but it still needs mowing.

The road to success
is always under repair.

We are not made rich by what is in our pockets but by what is in our hearts.

If you don't have
time to do it right,
when will you have
time to do it over?

It's often who you know that gets you there; it's what you know that keeps you there.

A bargain is often something you can't use at a price you can't resist.

Some people will believe anything, if you whisper it.

It is better to stumble than not to start.

No man knows his strengths who does not know his weaknesses.

The nice thing about teamwork is that you always have others on your side.

If you don't want anyone to know, don't do it.

Parents who never put their foot down usually have children who step on their toes.

Learn from the mistakes of others; you may not live long enough to make them all yourself.

People may doubt what you say, but they will believe what you do.

What may seem to be the end of the road may well be a new beginning.

Contentment is not the fulfillment of what you want, but the realization of how much you already have.

Doing nothing is tiresome - you can't stop and rest.

One of the most pleasant things about friendship is the "Do you remember" moments.

Whoever gossips
to you
will gossip of you.

The person who is pulling the oars doesn't have time to rock the boat.

It's not the size of the dog in the fight; it's the fight in the dog that's important.

The right to do
something does not
mean that doing it
is right.

Friends are the
family we can choose
for ourselves.

Old age is when most of the names in your little black book are doctors.

If you want to gather honey, don't kick over the beehive.

The smartest advice on raising children is to enjoy them while they're still on your side.

Don't think you are necessarily on the right track just because it's a well beaten path.

Good, better, best.
Never let it rest
until your good is
better and your better
is best.

Discipline is doing what doesn't come naturally.

The easiest way to
find something lost
is to buy a replacement.

Serving God is an investment that pays eternal dividends.

On contracts -
The large print
giveth and the small
print taketh away.

The mark of wise people is their ability to distinguish a setback from defeat.

Success is never
final
and failure never
fatal.

Religion may not keep you from sinning but it sure takes the joy out of it.

Being poor is a problem, but being rich isn't always the answer.

Keeping peace in the family requires patience, love, under-standing and at least two television sets.

Where you sit determines what you see.

Laughter is a tranquilizer with no side effects.

A good friend
doubles the joy
and divides the

Never speak ill of yourself. Others will always say enough on that subject.

The most important things in life aren't things.

It's tough to fly
with the eagles
in the morning
when you stay up
all night with the owls.

Misers aren't fun to live with but they make wonderful ancestors.

Some people are always grumbling that roses have thorns. Try to be a person that is thankful that thorns have roses.

Ask God's blessings on your work but don't ask him to do it for you.

Talk is cheap
because supply
always exceeds
the demand.

Don't lead me; I may not follow. Don't walk behind me; I may not lead. Walk beside me and be my friend.

When we get to the place where there's nothing left but God, we find He is enough.

When in doubt, don't!

I stood at the gate of life and said, "Give me a light that I may go safely into the unknown," and a voice replied, "Go into the darkness and put your hand into the hand of God. That will be to you better than a light and safer than a known way."

I'm delighted You want to know.

This all began with a different saying on the refrigerator door each week. When my oldest daughter graduated from college and left the nest, I said to her, "Carol, I want you to remember all those things I always told you." She yawned and said, "Yes, Mother, but maybe you'd better write them down."

So this book (and others) started out as a reminder of all the beautiful truths that had been passed down to me that I wanted to share with my children. What happened was that friends and relatives wanted copies, too. Soon I was in business assembling and selling books with the help of other members of my family. After several years of self-publishing, Thomas Nelson Publishers took on the job.

I hope you will share these wise words with others and the world will be a better place because of you.

Carolyn Coats

Published in Nashville, Tennessee, by Thomas Nelson, Inc., Publishers, and distributed
in Canada by Word Communications, Ltd., Richmond, British Columbia, and in the
United Kingdom by Word (UK), Ltd., Milton Keynes, England.

Library of Congress information

Coats, Carolyn, 1935-
    Things your Dad always told you, but you didn't want to hear / Carolyn Coats.
        p.   cm.
    Originally published: Orlando, Fla. : C. Coats, 1988.
    ISBN 0-7852-8055-3
    1. Quotations, English. 2. Proverbs. I. Title.
PN6081.C526 1994
818'.5402—dc20   93-38977
                                                                        CIP

Printed in the United States of America

1 2 3 4 5 6 7 - 99 98 97 96 95 94